DOGS: OUR BEST FRIENDS

BIG IDEAS: LOW INTERMEDIATE

KAREN RICHARDSON

WAYZGOOSE PRESS

CONTENTS

Edited by Robyn Brinks Lockwood

Cover design by Getcovers.com

Supplementary Materials

For Big Ideas downloadable learning tools for students and teachers, go to

https://www.wayzgoosepress.com/downloads/

INTRODUCTION

When you read an article or story, you have a conversation. The writer shares information, experiences, and ideas—but you, the reader, have your own ideas. When you read, you compare your experience and knowledge with the writer's ideas. Then you make decisions. Do you agree with the writer? Can you use the information to be healthier or more successful in your job, for example? Do you feel like the writer understands your life? Or do you learn about someone with a different point of view?

Because reading is a conversation, every reader experiences a text differently. When you read something interesting, you often want to talk about it. You want to share a similar experience, or you may want to argue. Maybe your friend understands the text in a different way. When you listen to your friend, you have a third set of ideas and experiences to compare to your own world view.

Big Ideas is designed to start interesting conversations between readers and writers, but also between readers and other readers. In this book about dogs, you'll learn about many types of dogs and what makes them so amazing. The chapters describe different breeds of dogs and what dogs can do and how they communicate. You will also learn about relationships between people and dogs, types of work dogs can do, and some famous and amazing dogs. There are always new and interesting questions and topics to explore.

While you learn about dogs, *Big Ideas* is also helping you develop language skills. Because our focus is on providing a positive reading experience, more than 90 percent of the words in this book are among the most common 2000 words in the English language. These are called "high frequency words." High frequency words appear over and over again in speaking and writing.

You might think it will be easy to learn high frequency words, and it is true that many words are easy. Content words, such as *tree, house, eat, drink,* and *blue* put a picture in your mind. They represent things you can see and name. They often have one meaning, and you can translate them easily.

However, many high frequency words change their meaning when they partner with other words in collocations. *Stay* is an example. When we say, *I stayed home yesterday,* then *stay* has a different meaning from *Let's try to stay awake all night* or *Stay away from the cake. I'm saving them for the party.* This flexibility shows that *stay* does not just have one meaning. It adapts to the words around it.

Fortunately, there is a method to learn the different meanings of collocations: read a lot. When you read, you see the words in different combinations, and you learn the meanings. This can happen naturally, but it will happen faster if you pay attention to words in groups. When you notice and highlight or copy word combinations, you can learn the different meanings.

You can also learn the grammar that goes with a vocabulary word. For example, you might see *educate* as a verb in *educate children*, *education* as a noun in *college education*, and *educational* as an adjective in an *educational experience*. Or, in another example, you can notice that some verbs are usually followed by a preposition, such as talk about or talk to, while others are followed by a noun as in *hear a bird*. These grammatical details are hard to hear in spoken English, but they are easy to spot in a written text.

While vocabulary has a strong relationship with grammar, grammar has a strong relationship with sentences. In order to give you a positive reading experience, we have worked hard to provide easy-to-read sentences. We use grammar from intermediate levels, and we reduce synonyms and idioms. Our goal is to keep the big ideas about dogs but present them in simple language. Since there are a lot of words related to dogs in this book, there is a section of words with short definitions and explanations at the beginning of the book. This section also includes some idioms related to dogs.

VOCABULARY

This book is for intermediate-level readers. Almost all the vocabulary is at the B1 level. However, when you read about dogs, some specialized vocabulary is needed, too.

You can learn these words before you read, or you can refer back to this section as necessary. You can also use a dictionary to check some words while you read or figure out what words mean by thinking about the rest of the sentence. However, we recommend reading through the example sentences and notes below before beginning the book, no matter what vocabulary strategy you use.

PARTS OF A DOG

- **fur**: the soft, thick hair of a dog. A *furry* dog is one that is covered in fur. *My young daughter loves to touch our dog's fur.*
- **paws**: a dog's feet. *Lily has three black paws and one white paw.*

- **tail:** the part that sticks out of the back end of a dog, which the dog can move from side to side. *Nala's long brown tail has a white tip.*

VERBS

- **bark:** A *bark* is a noun that describes the sound a dog makes. *My dog has a loud bark, but he's really very friendly. Bark* is also a regular verb: *The dog in that house barked all night.*
- **chew**: To bite on something again and again. *Our dog loves to chew on her bone after her evening dinner.*
- **growl**: The low sound made by a dog in the back of its throat as a warning. *The dog gave a warning growl when the man got too close.* The word *growl* can also be a verb that describes the action of making a growl: *The dog growled at the man.*
- **howl**: A long, loud call made by a dog or a wolf. *Our dog howls when my husband goes to work.*
- **lick**: To run your tongue over something, usually to taste or eat it. However, dogs also lick people to show affection or friendship. *My dog always licks my face when I get home.*
- **sniff**: To smell something: *My dog sniffed my hand after I ate the cookie. I think it smelled good to her!* The smell that dogs sniff for is called the **scent**: *The tracker dog sniffed the bag to get the scent. Then it followed the scent trail until it found the injured climber.* Dogs who sniff scents as part of their jobs are called *sniffer* dogs.

- **wag**: The movement that dogs make when it moves its tail from side to side. *Ivy always wags her tail when visitors arrive.*

- **collar:** a band of leather put around a dog's neck. Name tags or registration tags are often attached to a dog's collar. *Our dog has her name and telephone number on her collar.*
- **lead:** a long, thin piece of leather or a chain that you attach to a dog's collar to keep it under control. *Dogs must be kept on a lead in the park.* The American English word is *leash.*

A dog collar and lead

- **breed**: *Breed* can be a noun that refers to a group of dogs that look similar. *There are over 300 breeds of dog in the world.* The word can also be a verb. *To breed* means to mate and produce puppies. *Breed* is an irregular verb. The past tense is *bred.* A *breeder* is person who mates dogs for the purpose of producing puppies to sell.

- **companion**: An animal that spends a lot of time with you or travels with you, can be described as your companion. *Since Grandad died, Grandma's dearest companion is Bella, her Yorkshire terrier.*
- **cross**: a mixture of two (or more) different breeds of dog. *A* chorkie *is a cross between a chihuahua and a Yorkshire terrier. To cross* is a verb that describes the action of combining the two breeds of dog. *Sometimes two different breeds of dog are crossed on purpose to produce a new breed of dog.*
- **rescue dog**: a dog that has a new home after it was treated badly or left by its former owners. *Louie is a rescue dog. We adopted him from an animal shelter when he was four years old.*

NOTE

Although some people use *it* for animals, people who love dogs or have dogs as pets use *he* or *she* when talking about their dogs.

But what happens if you don't know the dog? What if you don't know if it is a male or female dog? Since we don't know the dogs in this book, we sometimes use *he* and sometimes use *she*.

PART ONE

ALL ABOUT DOGS

Dogs are one of the most popular animals to have as a pet. In this section, you will read a little history about dogs, various breeds, dog senses and abilities, and how dogs communicate.

CHAPTER 1

GENERAL BACKGROUND ABOUT DOGS

Why do we live with dogs? And more importantly, why do dogs want to live with us?

Dogs come from the Eurasian grey wolf, but dogs today are very different to wolves in both the way they look and the way they behave. Think of a dog like the Yorkshire terrier with its short legs, high bark, love of playing with a ball, and wearing pink or blue ribbons to keep the fur out of its eyes. It would be hard to find many similarities between these small family pets and the wolves that are slowly returning to the Tyrolean Alps of Austria and northern Italy. Around thirty-five thousand years ago, some wolves slowly started to change into dogs. The first proof scientists have that dogs lived and worked with humans comes from Neolithic times—around nine thousand years ago.

Early humans bred dogs for what they could do for people. Those people wanted good hunters, and dogs that could protect them and their sheep, goats, and other livestock animals. They also wanted their dogs to keep them warm. This is really not very different to what we want from dogs today. The phrase *a three-dog night* is said to come from the modern-day Aborigines in Australia, who on very cold nights would sleep with their dogs for the heat. The colder the night, the more dogs they needed to keep them warm.

More recently, people have carefully chosen dogs and bred them to change the way they look. They did this to make sure the dogs have features we think are cute or attractive, such as big eyes, short noses, and short legs. This breeding has caused health problems for certain dogs; for example, dogs whose legs are very short, whose noses are flat, or whose backs are too long.

But it's not only dog breeders who make money from dogs today. These days, businesses that deal with dogs bring a lot of money into our economy. How many dog services can you think of? People who buy a young puppy will need to train her. Puppy schools teach dogs how to socialise with other dogs, and teach their owners what a young dog needs and how to train her. Dog trainers and dog schools can help people who adopt an older dog that hasn't been trained well (or at all), or a rescue dog that might have special needs from an animal shelter.

It's not possible, or even a good idea, to take dogs with you everywhere you go. Most dogs can be left alone for a few hours, but if you are going out for the whole day or evening, you might need a dog sitter. Like a babysitter for children, dog sitters look after your dog. If you need to leave your dog overnight or while you are away on holiday or business, then you might need to take your dog to a boarding kennel or dog hotel. There are even doggy day care centres that will look after your dog while you are at work. Some have dog cams (like baby monitoring cameras) and live video feeds so that you can see what your dog is doing while you are at work. An option that is a little less expensive is a dog walker for dogs who are alone at home for a few hours. A dog walker comes and takes your dog for a walk, probably together with one or two other dogs, while you are at work.

There are places that provide services such as bathing and washing your dog, cutting its long fur, and trimming its claws. What would a wolf think about a dog spa or resort? Life has certainly changed a lot for dogs over the past few thousand years.

How old is your eleven-year-old dog in human years? Is your eleven-month-old puppy already a teenager? In the past, people said that each dog year was the same as seven human years. However, this is not true. Now people know a twelve-month-old medium-sized dog is about 15 years old in human years. So yes, your eleven-month-old puppy is a teenager, and that might explain why he doesn't always go to bed when you tell him to, and instead runs around in a happy and excited way. A dog's second year of life is about the same as nine human years. After that, each year is about five human years. This calculation is not as complicated as it sounds. To calculate the age of an eleven-year-old dog, just add 15 (for his first year) + 9 (for his second year) + 9 x 5 (for each of the next nine years) to equal approximately 69 human years. However, this is an approximate age because small dogs generally live longer than larger dogs. In any case, just like humans, dogs are able to live longer these days because they eat better food, get better health care, and hopefully live in a warm, safe home with people who love and care for them.

REFLECTION

1. Find out what dog services are available where you
   live. What do they cost? What special services do
   they offer?
2. What are some reasons people like dogs? Do you
   know anyone who does not like dogs? Why don't
   they like dogs?

CHAPTER 2

DOG BREEDS

How many different breeds of dog are there? This is a difficult question to answer. According to the American Kennel Club (AKC), there are about 200 different breeds, but this number is increasing all the time. The World Canine Association, also known as the Fédération Cynologique Internationale (FCI), recognises 356 breeds.

Of course, there are many accidental mixed breeds too: dogs that have parents and grandparents from different breeds. Some dogs are so mixed that it's impossible to tell what kind of dog they are by looking at them.

Sometimes dogs are crossed on purpose to produce a new breed of dog with special characteristics or qualities. These cross-breeds are sometimes known as 'designer dogs' and include new breeds such as the *labradoodle*, a cross between a Labrador retriever and a poodle, or the *chorkie*, a cross between a chihuahua and a Yorkshire terrier.

There are seven dog breed groups recognised by the American Kennel Club:

- sporting
- hound
- working
- terrier
- toy
- herding
- non-sporting

Sporting breeds were bred to help hunters. They are good at catching and bringing back ducks and other birds. They are happy to go into water, and they usually have thick fur. Dogs that belong to the sporting group include spaniels and retrievers.

A golden retriever

Hounds also help hunters, but they chase and catch (mostly) small animals such as rabbits, hare, and sometimes deer. This group includes the sighthounds with their long legs and fast speed. Many dogs in this group have *hound* in their name, such as

A basset hound

foxhound, greyhound, bloodhound, basset hound, and wolfhound.

A fox terrier

Terriers were also bred to help humans, not to hunt animals for food, but to catch and kill animals people don't want around, such as mice, rats, and other vermin. These dogs are generally small with short legs and can find and dig out animals that hide underground in small holes. Well-known breeds in this group are bull terriers, (Jack) Russell terriers, and fox terriers.

Herding dogs are good at moving farm animals, such as sheep and cows, about the farm. These dogs are intelligent and can be trained to do what the farmer wants them to do. Because they are easy to train and loyal to their humans, police dogs are part of this group. Border collies, Australian shepherds, and German shepherds are also included in this group. Perhaps surprisingly, corgis are part of this group.

A German shepherd

Working group dogs do all the other work. They pull sleds

and carts, they guard people, and they look after buildings and other animals. Dogs in the working group are strong and intelligent. The Maremma, a live-stock guardian dog, has white fur so that it can hide among the sheep and keep them safe from

A mastiff

wolves and bears. Other more well-known working dogs and guard dogs include Rottweilers, mastiffs, and huskies.

Toy dogs are small dogs that were bred to live with people and to be compan-ions. It's almost impossible to be lonely when a toy dog is around. Toy breeds are good dogs for people who live in towns and cities because they are happy to go to the park and don't need long walks and as much exercise as dogs from other groups. Toy dogs are

A chihuahua

popular with celebrities and others who like to dress dogs in clothing and carry them around. Breeds in this group include pugs, chihuahuas, and Yorkshire terriers.

Non-sporting is the name for a group of dogs that don't really fit into the other groups. They may be large or small, but they are usually dogs that live well in homes with people

and are not working dogs. This group includes popular breeds such as Dalmatians, poodles, French bulldogs, the Shiba Inu from Japan, and Chinese chow-chows.

A Dalmatian

We often connect certain breeds of dog with certain people. Picture the late Queen Elizabeth II of the United Kingdom. Which breed of dog do you connect with her? It's probably the corgi.

A corgi running in the park

REFLECTION

1. What breeds do you think are the most interesting? Why? Do you know anybody who owns a dog? What breed do they own?

2. Which breeds of dog could happily live in a family house with young children? Which breed of dog might be a good companion for a single person in their 70s? Explain your choices.

CHAPTER 3

DOG SENSES AND ABILITIES

SMELL

Dogs have an amazing sense of smell. Although dogs' brains are smaller than human brains, the part of a dog's brain that controls smell is comparatively about forty times larger than the part of our brain that controls smell.

Smell is extremely important to dogs. When you see a dog sniffing around the park, he's probably just smelling to find out which dogs have already been to the park that day, which dogs walked past his house, and which were friendly.

Dogs are naturally very interested in new smells. That's why they can be trained to smell new scents connected with new human diseases such as Covid. During the pandemic, dogs worked at airports to smell and recognise people who had the virus. There are also experiments going on at the moment to find out how well dogs can smell other diseases like cancer, diabetes, and malaria.

Unlike humans, dogs can move their noses and their nostrils. This movement helps them decide which direction the new smell is coming from, and helps them track criminals and missing people, such as small children and people with dementia. Dog breeds that are especially good at sniffing and making the most of their sense of smell are hounds, such as bloodhounds.

See Chapters 9 and 10 for more information and stories about dogs and their amazing sense of smell.

SIGHT

Dogs can see better in the dark than humans can, but they can't see colour very well. Dogs see the world in shades of grey, with a bit of blue and yellow. Dog toys are often yellow and blue because these are the colours a dog can see best. Red, green, orange, purple, and brown all look like shades of grey to a dog. It's a little bit like a person being colour-blind.

Dogs can see us better when we move. So, if people want to get their dog's attention, they should try waving to it. This is also the reason why dogs can be trained to respond to hand signals.

Sighthounds, such as greyhounds, the galgo Español (Spanish greyhound), whippets, salukis, and Irish wolfhounds hunt by sight and speed. They can see slightly better and further than other types of dogs and are better at noticing movement. This is why they are still today used as hunting and racing dogs in many parts of the world. Sadly, this is also why the poor Spanish galgos are often treated very badly and thrown away when they are around three years old and no longer as fast and agile as younger dogs. Sighthounds are usually thin, have long legs, and a deep chest. All these characteristics help them to run very fast. A greyhound can easily reach speeds of 65-70 kilometres an hour.

HEARING

Dogs have incredible hearing. They can hear a much larger range of sounds than humans–up to sixty thousand hertz. Humans can only hear between twelve and twenty thousand hertz. That's why dogs can hear sounds such as dog whistles that we cannot hear. Dogs can hear about four times better than people can, so imagine how loud some of our human noises are to dogs, such as vacuum cleaners, doorbells, and alarm clocks. It's not surprising that dogs are often very scared of loud fireworks.

Dogs have 18 muscles in their ears, and they can move their ears in the direction of a sound. When people try this, it's impossible. People do have muscles in their ears, but over time they have forgotten how to use them.

Just like people, dogs can start to lose their hearing and sight when they get old. Many old dogs get cataracts in their eyes. So, if you meet a dog with cloudy grey eyes, talk to him in a friendly voice because he might not be able to see you very well.

REFLECTION

1. What are some things that dogs can do better than people because of their senses?
2. What can people do to make their home and garden safe and comfortable for old dogs who can no longer see or hear very well?

Chapter 4

Dog Communication

Dogs communicate with each other, and they communicate with us. Dogs that live with people are watching all the time. They know what human voices mean, and they know what many of people's movements mean. Very often dogs understand people better than people understand dogs.

Like people, dogs communicate with their voices and with their bodies. Ears are very important to how a dog communicates. Looking at a dog's ears can often help someone understand how the dog is feeling.

When a dog holds his ears naturally, he is probably feeling relaxed and comfortable. If he raises his ears, it means he heard something that interests him. He will probably turn his body towards the sound too. But if he holds his ears up and forward, he is showing that he is angry and might attack. Ears that are pulled back (but not held flat to the head) show that the dog is friendly. If a dog pulls back his ears and puts them down flat onto his head, then he probably feels frightened or afraid.

In the past, some dog owners clipped or cut a dog's ears or its tail. They thought this made it look better. Thankfully, cutting is no longer allowed or legal in most countries. If someone cuts a dog's ears or its tail, then it cannot communicate properly, and it might even make the dog angry enough to bite.

Many people believe that when a dog wags its tail, he is happy. That's only partly true. Dogs often do wag their tails when they are happy, such as when they greet people, but they also wag their tails when they are scared. A high wag is often a happy wag, and a low wagging tail is often an unhappy wag. It depends what else the dog is doing.

What about when a dog opens its mouth wide and yawns? Does that mean he is tired? Again, the answer is both yes and no. A dog will often yawn when he doesn't understand what you want from him. He can't understand you, so he shows that by yawning.

A dog that is feeling a little bit worried will yawn, blink his eyes, and maybe lick his nose with his tongue. When he gets more worried, he might turn his head away. If the person still doesn't understand him and do what the dog wants, the next thing the dog will do is turn his whole body away. He might then sit and lift his paw. If the person still doesn't understand, the dog will try to leave the situation that is making it uncomfortable. He will try to walk away. If the dog cannot do this, perhaps because he is on a short lead, it might put his tail between his legs. If the dog is still scared, and no one helps him or allows him to leave the situation, the dog will probably growl. A person should not ignore what this dog is trying to say because the next thing he might do is bite! It's not the dog's fault. The dog has been trying to say that he's unhappy or scared. For safety and for the well-being of the dogs, people really should learn to understand what dogs are trying to say.

A growl doesn't always lead to a bite. A dog that's happily playing with another dog might growl, but this is just part of the game. It's not anger. However, a dog may also growl at another dog to tell them, "Go away, leave me alone, that's my toy, and you're not having it."

There are many books, videos, and websites that can help people understand dog communication. Doggone Safe is a US-based non-profit organization that tries to educate adults and children about dog behaviour, how to act around dogs, and how to stay safe. It teaches children, for example, to "be a tree"—to stand still with their arms straight down against their body. A dog will nearly always think this is boring and go away. Being a tree is one way to stay safe.

However, young children should never be left alone with any dog because even the friendliest dog can bite or pretend to bite when he's tired of a child pulling it ears or tail, being too loud, or making sudden movements.

Dogs often use their eyebrows to communicate with their owners. When dogs try to communicate messages, such as "Don't leave me" or "Take me for a walk," they often raise their eyebrows and tilt their head slightly. Recent academic research tells us what dog owners already know: that dogs change their facial expressions to get love and understanding. The research shows that dogs in animal shelters who make their eyes wide and raise their eyebrows when people come to visit get adopted more quickly and get a new home. This action is where the phrase *making puppy dog eyes* comes from.

Reflection

1. How else do dogs communicate with people or with other dogs?
2. What should people do or not do when they meet new dogs?

PART TWO

DOGS AND US

In this section, you will read about how important we are to
dogs, how important they are to us, and what we can do to

make sure this relationship is a happy and healthy one—for both dog and human.

CHAPTER 5

DOGS AND HUMAN HEALTH & WELL-BEING

According to the American Veterinary Medical Association, nearly 40 percent of homes in the United States own at least one pet dog, and many homes have two or more dogs. People in the United Kingdom, which is sometimes called a country of animal lovers, had over ten million pet dogs in 2022, with 27 percent of adults in the United Kingdom owning a dog. Australia is even more dog-friendly and has one of the highest percentages of dog ownership in the world. According to the Royal Society for the Prevention of Cruelty to Animals (RSPCA) in Australia, there is at least one dog living in 48 percent of all Australian homes.

Dogs can be expensive. Food, health care, and all the equipment and accessories a dog needs, such as leads, collars, harnesses, beds, food bowls, and toys, are not cheap. So why do so many people own a dog?

One of the main reasons is companionship. The meaning of this is clear in the words other languages have for the English word *pet*. In Spanish, the word can be *animal de compañía* (as well as *mascota*). In French, people usually say *animal de compagnie.* The Romanians use the same phrase with a different spelling: *animal de companie.* People like the company of dogs. Dogs give us love and affection. Think about who is happier to see you when you get home from the supermarket or work—your family or your dog?

This is, of course, not a one-way relationship. People also love their dogs, and this is good for personal growth. Many studies show that children who grow up in a house where the pet dog is an important part of the family grow into more caring adults.

Studies also show that children who grow up with dogs spend more time out in the fresh air. In a time when much of children's lives are spent indoors or looking at a screen, being with animals outside in the fresh air can have positive long-term effects on their mental and physical health. Playing ball games outside on a sunny day with a happy dog is a simple pleasure that children will probably remember for the rest of their lives.

And it's not only children who benefit from living with a dog. Adults who have dogs are more likely to walk in the woods or on the beach and connect with nature. People who walk, for example, along the side of a river every day are more likely to notice how nature changes day by day and with the different seasons. They will see which flowers, trees, and mushrooms grow at certain times, hear birds sing, and discover which animals live in their area. Daily walks with a dog outside in the fresh air and in all types of weather help strengthen our general health, which means fewer colds and other illnesses. And of course, the act of walking is good for our knees, our bodies, our general fitness, and our figures.

It is amazing how many people say "Hello" and "Good morning" to people who are walking dogs. They even stop and talk or ask questions about the dog. Try sitting in a park with a friendly dog and see how long it takes for someone to ask about the dog. Dogs—especially friendly dogs—increase the amount of social contact their owners have. Many people who get a dog soon start to walk their dogs with other dog owners and their dogs. They might join a dog club, attend a training course, or go to a puppy school where they meet other dog owners. It's easy for dog owners to make new friends.

Studies show that being with a calm dog and stroking or petting him can lower blood pressure and reduce stress levels. Dogs sit with people when they are sad. After people have an illness or operation, dogs make them get up and go outside sooner, which helps them heal more quickly.

Some people who have mental health problems say that they often feel better when they are with an animal. Any animal can be an *Emotional Support Animal* (ESA), but most ESAs are dogs. ESAs do not need to have special training, but if their owner needs to always have their ESA with them a doctor can write a letter so that the animal can be registered as an ESA. Registered ESAs can go into restaurants and even travel on planes with their owners.

Therapy dogs usually have a certificate that says they are calm and social animals that are not scared of loud noises or sudden movements. A therapy dog does not have to be registered, and he does not just help one person. Therapy dogs (and cats) can bring comfort and support to people in care homes, children in special schools, and people who have lived through a difficult situation or event, such as a shooting or an attack.

There is a disadvantage to dogs being such important members of the family when a couple breaks up or divorces.

These days, there are not only legal cases about who the children live with after a divorce, there are also court cases and legal battles about who keeps the dog.

REFLECTION

1. Can we really "own" a dog? Is a dog property like a house or a table?
2. In which ways can dogs bring comfort and support to people who need it?

CHAPTER 6

DOGS AND THEIR RIGHTS

Dogs help improve our mental and physical health so it's important that owners make sure their dogs are getting a good quality of life in return.

The United Kingdom Animal Welfare Act of 2006, which is now part of a law, says that dogs have five main needs: suitable diet, suitable living environment, appropriate companionship, good health, and the opportunity to behave normally.

A SUITABLE DIET

A *suitable diet* means the right food for the right size and breed of dog. It also means the right amount of food, so that the dog does not go hungry but also does not become overweight. Either too little food or too much food can cause other health problems. The dog should get food that contains all the vitamins and minerals she needs each day. Food meant for people might not be good for dogs. Many things people eat can make dogs ill, such as onions, grapes, and chocolate. Some of our foods are even poisonous to dogs. Like human babies need baby food, puppies need special food. And like elderly people who aren't as active or fit as they used to be, older dogs often need food that is softer and has fewer calories and more vitamins. All dogs must always have access to fresh, clean water to drink.

A SUITABLE LIVING ENVIRONMENT

A dog has the right to a safe place to live. He should not be able to jump through an open window, fall off a balcony, or run out to a road where there are cars and other dangers. Dogs should not be kept in places that are too hot, too cold, or too small for them to move. He should have a bed of his own to sleep in and a safe quiet place he can go to when he wants to be by himself. A dog needs a toilet area, and there should be no poisonous plants outside or inside that he might accidently eat.

THE RIGHT TO APPROPRIATE COMPANIONSHIP

There are many reasons why it might not be possible for a dog owner to have more than one dog at a time. However, dogs need, and have the right, to regularly be with other friendly dogs. This might mean the owner needs to take a dog to a (dog) park where he can play off the lead with other dogs, or to go on walks with other dogs.

Most dogs can be trained to stay alone at home for up to four hours, which is the longest time that experts recommend. Very young, very old, or very nervous dogs should be left alone even less than four hours. Some dogs will develop behaviour problems when they are left on their own. They might bark, howl, or chew things they shouldn't chew. Some people who got a dog during the Covid pandemic had difficulties when they returned to work. The dogs developed behaviour problems because they lost their companion. This situation sadly resulted in many dogs being returned to dog shelters. Doggy day care or a regular dog walker are two solutions, but they can be expensive.

The Right to Be Kept in Good Health

A dog may not always be able to let its owner know when he feels ill or when he is in pain. Therefore, it is important that all dogs go to a veterinarian, also called a vet (pet doctor) to have regular health checks.

At a preventative health check, a vet will look at the dog's teeth, listen to his heart and chest, look into his ears and eyes, check his legs and paws, and cut his claws if they are too long. At these appointments, dogs can get their regular vaccinations to stop them from getting and spreading diseases.

The Opportunity to Be Able to Behave Normally

Normal behaviour means to behave like a dog. All dogs need exercise, though some dogs need more than others. But whatever their size and age, dogs should go on regular walks where they are allowed to sniff, explore, and investigate the outside world. Dogs like to play and run, so if possible, they should have time off the lead with other dogs that they like.

Like children, dogs might have favourite toys. Allowing them to play with these toys at home will prevent them from becoming bored and unhappy. Behaving normally does not mean being uncontrolled. Therefore, it is important to train a dog using rewards and not punishments.

Do you know these basic dog commands in English? What are they in your language? Do you know how to tell your dog he did a good job when he followed your command?

- Come:
- Sit:
- Stay:
- Down:
- Bring/Fetch:
- Drop it:
- Wait:
- Heel:
- Good boy/Good girl:
- Good dog:

The law in many countries says that dogs must be *microchipped*. To do this, a vet uses a needle to insert a small microchip under the dog's skin, usually between its shoulders. The chip is then registered on a database. The microchip can help identify a dog that is lost or has been stolen, so that he can be returned to its owners. Like people, dogs need a passport to travel to a different country. The microchip number is included on the dog's passport.

REFLECTION

1. Should all dogs be kept on a lead in towns and cities? Why or why not? If you think dogs should be let off their lead, should every town or city provide

a dog park where dogs can be let off the lead? What are some pros and cons?

2. Where do people in your community get dogs from? Think of all the different kinds of places. What are some advantages and disadvantages to each?

CHAPTER 7

GUIDE DOGS

Losing your sight or your ability to see well is a major life change, but one that can be made a little bit easier with a specially trained dog at your side. In the United Kingdom, these dogs are called *guide dogs*; in the United States, they are more commonly called *seeing-eye dogs*. Guide dogs help humans who are blind or partially sighted to live more independent lives. The dogs help their owners walk around town centres, use public transport, and go to work by themselves, so that they do not have to depend on their family and friends.

Golden retrievers, Labradors, German shepherds, and some poodles are all breeds that are good guide dogs. Fifty percent of guide dogs in the United Kingdom are Golden retrievers crossed either with a Labrador or German shepherd.

Not everyone who wants a guide dog can get one. The person is carefully checked so that the right guide dog can be found for their special needs. It doesn't matter how young or old the person is. There is no age limit, but the owner must be able to look after the dog. People cannot buy a guide dog. The dogs usually come from a charity.

When a puppy has passed the guide dog test and is chosen to be trained as a guide dog, he first goes to a puppy walker. This walker is often someone who has a family with children. The puppy stays with them until it is just over a year old. During this time, it gets normal dog training and is closely watched to see whether it will make a good, reliable guide dog. Not all puppies stay in the program. Some do not pay attention to their trainers, do not get along with other dogs, or develop health problems. Although they might not be good guide dogs, these dogs usually make very good pets. They are taken out of the training program and can start a new life as a family dog in a loving home.

The dogs that stay in the program are trained by expert trainers and are only matched with their new owner once the guide dog training is completed successfully. Then both the dog and new owner get new partnership training. This training might be a 10-day course, where the dog and owner live together and get to know each other, and the owner learns how to look after the dog. Further training for both the dog and owner takes place at the owner's home, where the dog learns the routes the owner needs to take and gets to know the owner's home and workplace. Further training and support usually last about another year. All of this training takes a lot of time and money.

The full cost of training a guide dog from birth to when they are too old to continue working is around £55,000 in the United Kingdom or around $60,000 in the United States, so it is really important that the dog is the right dog for the training and its future job. In 2023, there were currently around 5,000 working guide dogs in the United Kingdom and over 10,000 in the United States, according to the non-profit organisation Guiding Eyes for the Blind.

A guide dog makes sure that its owner walks in the middle of the pavement or sidewalk and does not get too close to the road. He stops when he comes to a road, and makes sure the owner walks across the road in a straight line. The dog goes around holes and things that are in the way and might be dangerous, and he makes sure the owner does not hit their head. A guide dog will not turn a corner unless his owner tells it to. The owner is always the boss in the partnership and must tell the guide dog what they want him to do and where they want him to go.

Although guide dogs do a job, they still have the same rights as other dogs. That means they must get regular exercise, have time to play, get proper food and health care, be told they are a 'good girl' or 'good boy', and get rewards when they do a good job. Like all workers, guide dogs are allowed to retire when they get old. This usually happen when the dog is between the ages of 8 and 11.

Did you know that there are not only guide dogs but also hearing (or signal) dogs? These dogs are trained to help adults and children who cannot hear. Some things hearing dogs can do is to tell their owner when the doorbell rings or when a smoke alarm goes off. They can also let their owners know that someone is calling their name or that the alarm clock is ringing and it's time to get up.

REFLECTION

1. What features and qualities do you think a dog needs to become a guide dog or hearing dog? Explain your answer.
2. How might a seeing-eye or hearing dog save its owner's life?

PART THREE

WORKING DOGS

Not all dogs are family pets. Many dogs are trained to do a special job. In this section, you will read about some of these

8

8 KAREN RICHARDSON

dogs and the work they do to help and protect people and
other animals.

CHAPTER 8

FARM DOGS

Good working sheepdogs are often a farmer's best friend and helper. Border collies are very intelligent dogs and make particularly good working farm dogs. They are quick and happy to learn, healthy, fast, and full of energy. For these reasons, they can be difficult to keep as a family pet because they need a lot of attention and mental stimulation, always want things to do, and need at least three hours of physical exercise a day.

When people imagine working sheepdogs, they probably think of black and white border collies. These dogs originally come from the border area between northern England and Scotland, which is how they got their name. But there are many other sheepdog breeds around the world, including the popular Australian shepherd dog, the German shepherd, the Belgian shepherd, the Dutch shepherd, the Icelandic sheep-dog, and the Old English sheepdog. There are also some breeds that people don't think of when they think about working farm dogs. These include the Welsh corgi. Despite its short legs, its deep bark, and strong personality, the corgi is good at herding both sheep and cattle.

Sheepdog trials are competitions that show how good a dog is at controlling and moving sheep. Sheepdog trials started in New Zealand in the 1860s and soon became popular in parts of the United Kingdom. Today they are popular events around the world, but the best places to see a sheepdog trial are New Zealand, Australia, Ireland, and the United Kingdom. The most common breed of dog in these competitions is still the black and white border collie who works in very close contact with its owner.

Guardian dogs also work with farmers and farm animals, but they have a very different job. Instead of running around and moving the sheep, they often stand still in the middle of a flock of sheep so that they can protect the sheep without being seen from far away. An example of a guardian dog is the large, white, furry Maremmano-Abruzzese from Italy. This dog, which looks a bit like a large sheep, has been used for hundreds of years by mountain farmers to protect their sheep from wolves and bears. Maremmano puppies grow up with sheep, so they get used to them very quickly.

There are many valuable things on a farm, and so many farms have larger dogs that work as guard dogs. Smaller dogs can control and decrease the number of rats. Jack Russell terriers and dachshunds are particularly good at rat control.

REFLECTION

1. Why might a dog be a better farm employee than a human? Support your answer.

2. Can, or should, working farm dogs be pets? Why or why not?

CHAPTER 9

AIRPORT DOGS

Sniffer dogs help to make flying safe and can even make airport waiting times shorter. Sniffer dogs have been employed by the military, and they have worked at airports for many years, sniffing out and detecting dangerous things such as bombs and explosives. If the airport receives a report that someone saw something suspicious while boarding a plane, dogs that are especially trained to sniff out bombs and explosives go onto the planes to check. Whether on a plane or at the airport, a bag that doesn't seem right and has no one with it does not have to be opened to check whether it's safe or not. Sniffer dogs can detect many smells through plastic, metal, and leather. And they can detect smells within smells; for example, they can even detect drugs hidden inside a jar of strong-smelling coffee.

The increase in airport and plane-related terrorism in the 1970s, and after the 9/11 New York terrorist attacks, made the work of airport dogs even more important. Many people in the United States first learned about sniffer dogs after a German shepherd named Brandy sniffed out a bomb on a

TWA plane at a New York airport in 1972, just minutes before it was due to explode. The passengers were already on the plane, so Brandy stopped a terrible disaster and saved many lives that day.

Airport dogs also sniff out and find illegal items that passengers are not allowed to carry onto a plane, such as drugs, plants, seeds, large amounts of money, guns, forbidden animal parts like ivory and rhinoceros horn, and even living animals, such as snakes and other reptiles, that are sometimes hidden in cases and bags.

Airports in the United States currently employ around 1,000 sniffer dogs. The dogs work in teams with their handlers (people who train and control dogs). These days, we are used to seeing sniffer dogs at airports, and it doesn't worry passengers. In fact, passengers are often less nervous when they see a sniffer dog than when they see police officers with machine guns and bullet-proof vests walking about the airport.

If an unattended bag is found at an airport, a sign from a sniffer dog that the bag is safe can prevent everyone from leaving the airport. Thanks to the sniffer dog, passengers will not have to leave the building, and their holidays, meetings, and other travel can go ahead as planned.

Sniffer dogs do not only work at airports. They do the same job on ferries, trains, and other forms of transport, so they also work at ports and railway stations. They often work at places where there are large crowds of people, like football matches, the Olympic Games, and concerts and music festivals.

Helsinki Airport in Finland was one of the first international airports to use sniffer dogs during the Covid pandemic. The dogs were specially trained to detect passengers who had the Covid virus. These passengers could then be stopped before they got onto their plane and infected the other passengers and crew. Reports say that the dogs were successful at sniffing out Covid infections 80% to 100% of the time. There is now a new term used to describe these dogs: *Biomedical Detection Dogs*, or BMDDs.

The most common breeds of dog trained as sniffer dogs are spaniels, retrievers, bloodhounds, beagles, German shepherds, and Belgian Malinois.

Some electronics companies have tried to create a robot to do the work of a sniffer dog. But why should airport security firms spend all that money on a piece of metal to do something that comes naturally to a dog? Surveys show that passengers feel safer and less worried about flying when they see sniffer dogs at work in an airport. Would they say the same thing about a robot sniffer dog replacement?

REFLECTION

1. What benefits do sniffer dogs have over bomb detection robots? What advantages do bomb detection robots have over sniffer dogs?
2. Where else do you think sniffer dogs could be employed? Why do you think so?

CHAPTER 10

SEARCH AND RESCUE DOGS

Dogs are not only good at sniffing out and finding bombs, drugs, and other illegal things, they are also experts at sniffing out and finding missing people and bodies.

Search and rescue dogs recently found at least 39 people who were buried under buildings that collapsed in the terrible earthquake that hit Turkey and Syria in February 2023. Search and rescue dogs with their handlers went to the earthquake areas as soon as it was possible. The teams came from all over the world, including some as far away as Switzerland, India, and Mexico. Some of the buildings that fell down were 14 floors high, so the bricks, cement, and other building materials made too big a pile for humans to hear people trapped underneath. But search and rescue dogs with their amazing sense of smell were able to find many people who were still alive and save them.

The dogs are trained to sniff out the human scent. They can do this even if someone is under eight or nine metres of bricks and other building materials. Their handlers send them to run around over the bricks and into places too small or dangerous for human rescuers. When a search and rescue dog smells a human underneath the building, it stops and barks to tell his handler. A second dog is usually sent to confirm the scent before people start digging to find the person.

When a search and rescue dog (sometimes called a REDOG) finds a person, they get something to eat or a toy as a reward. The dogs work for many hours a day, usually for 20 minutes each hour, with a 40-minute break. The dog needs to have a lot of energy and not get tired quickly.

The work can be dangerous for the dogs too. Proteo, a German shepherd search and rescue dog from a Mexican team, was killed in Kahramanmaras in Turkey in 2023 when a building fell on him while he was searching for people buried under buildings after the earthquake. Proteo had already helped rescue three people in the days before he died. Proteo's body was returned Mexico, where he was called a hero. There are plans to put up a statue of Proteo in Turkey.

Search and rescue dogs do not only work after earth-quakes. They also help find people after other natural disasters such as avalanches, when large amounts of snow fall down a mountain, or after man-made disasters like plane crashes or bombings.

The first known avalanche dogs were Saint Bernard dogs in the 1700s. These large dogs with their thick warm fur accompanied monks (men who belong to a religious group and usually live together in building called a *monastery*) in the snowy mountains in Switzerland when they walked from monastery to monastery. Today, German shepherds, Labradors, and spaniels are just as likely to be used as avalanche dogs or mountain rescue dogs, but many people still picture a friendly St. Bernard with a small barrel of brandy attached to its collar. With modern advances in technology, an avalanche dog might seem old-fashioned; but again, dogs are still doing a better job than robots. And with climate change causing more avalanches in the mountains, we now need more, not fewer, avalanche and mountain rescue dogs.

As with sniffer dogs, robots are being designed to do the work of search and rescue dogs, but dogs still have many advantages over robots: they do not need someone to operate them, they do not need an internet connection or a battery, and they do not need to be built because they are already here and ready to work. And, most importantly, the dog's sense of smell is still better than that of the robot.

Even when there is no possibility of finding survivors, search and rescue dogs can give us hope. An American Kennel Club exhibition in New York in 2021 provided information and showed photos of the work of search and rescue dogs, including Trakr, a German shepherd; Riley, a golden retriever; and Ricky, a small rat terrier. These dogs continued to search under the bricks and building materials for two weeks after the 9/11 terrorist attack on the World Trade Center buildings in New York. Although they did not find any people still alive, they found the bodies of many people, and they were a great help and comfort to the human rescuers. Even many years after the attack, people are still talking and learning about the brave and hard-working search and rescue dogs.

REFLECTION

1. Which would you prefer to be rescued by—a search and rescue dog or a robot? Why? How could search and rescue dogs and robots work together?
2. What dangers and other problems might search and rescue dogs and their handlers meet in their work?

PART FOUR

AMAZING DOG STORIES

A statue in New Zealand honouring sheepdogs

All dogs are special in their own way, but some dogs are extra special. In this section, you will read about some amazing dogs. Some of them are famous for what they did, and some just for who they are.

CHAPTER 11

DUKE AND MAX: THE MAYORS

Dogs have had some very unusual jobs. Duke was a Great Pyrenees and a great dog. At least, that's what voters in Cormorant Village in Minnesota in the United States thought.

Duke lived in the village with his owners. He was such a popular dog that the people of the village made him their mayor (the head of a town or a city). And the voters elected him four times! He was first elected mayor in 2014. By 2016, he received nearly 100% of the votes in the election for mayor. He only lost one vote, and that was to another dog named Lassie.

A Great Pyrenees dog the same color as Duke (but not Duke himself)

Luckily, Duke did not have to make any decisions. He spent a lot of time hanging out at the local pub, watching what was going on in the village. His jobs as mayor included leading celebrations and promoting the village. His photo was put up on bill-boards. After four years as mayor, Duke retired at the age of

13. Sadly, he died soon afterwards. Although Cormorant is a very small village, its large, white, furry mayor made it famous all over the United States.

Amazingly, Duke was not the only dog who was mayor of a town or village. Maximus Mighty-Dog Mueller the Second was more often known by a shorter name, Mayor Max the Second. Mayor Max II, a golden retriever, was elected mayor in the town of Idyllwild-Pine Cove in California. Idyllwild is a mountain resort that is popular with artists and musicians. The town is unincorporated, which means it has no local government. Therefore, the people who live there can elect whoever and whatever they want to be their mayor. In 2012, to raise money for a local animal shelter, people who lived in the town were told they could enter their cats and dogs into an election for mayor. A golden retriever called Max won the election.

Sadly, he died less than a year later, and so another golden retriever, Mayor Max II, took his place. Mayor Max II kept his job as mayor for nine years until he died in 2022. Like Duke in Cormorant Village, Max's job was to represent and promote the town, and to welcome visitors. He did his job so well that he became known all over the world.

Idyllwild's new mayor started his job in December 2022 at the very young age of three months old. Unsurprisingly, he is a golden retriever, and his name is Mayor Max the Third. Hopefully he will stay in his job as the mayor of Idyllwild for many years.

REFLECTION

1. Why do you think the people of Cormorant Village and Idyllwild decided to elect a dog, and not a person, as their mayor? Would you vote for a dog instead of a person? Why or why not?
2. What breed of dog would be a good representative for your city, town, or village? Why?

CHAPTER 12

LASSIE: THE HOLLYWOOD STAR

Lassie is one of the most famous dog television stars. Even if you haven't seen a Lassie film or TV show, you may have heard the name "Lassie." The original *Lassie* films are really old now, but many people still call brown and white collie dogs "Lassie dogs." Lassie is probably still the world's best-known film and TV dog, a famous dog who has a star on the Hollywood Walk of Fame in Los Angeles.

Lassie started out as the main character in a 1940 novel by Eric Knight. The movie company Metro-Goldwyn-Meyer (MGM) made the story into a film in 1943 called *Lassie Come Home*. In the film, the female dog Lassie was played by a male collie dog named Pal.

Around 1,500 dogs tried out for the role of Lassie. Pal was very good, but MGM didn't want him because he was a male dog. Pal was first only hired to do some of the difficult parts of the action that the female dog didn't want to do. Pal was so good and brave doing these things that he took over the lead role as Lassie. Pal went on to star in another six Lassie movies until the early 1950s. The films were so popular that MGM decided to film them in colour at a time when many big films were still made in black and white.

A collie

The first episodes of the *Lassie* TV shows were filmed in 1954. Pal also starred in the first two pilot episodes before he retired. Pal died in 1958, but his descendants—his children and children's children—have been playing the role of Lassie in TV shows and films ever since. The TV series *Lassie* ran from 1954 to 1973. During this time, Lassie was played by five dogs, who were all male and all descendants of the original Lassie actor, Pal.

Since then, other male dogs not related to Pal have played Lassie. The reason why Lassie has always been played on film by male dogs is that males are bigger and have thicker fur, so they look more impressive on screen.

REFLECTION

1. What other famous dogs from television or movies do you know or can you find online? What did they star in? What kinds of dogs were they?
2. Do a quick online search. How many other dogs have a star on the Hollywood Walk of Fame? What are their names? What are they famous for?

CHAPTER 13

BALTO: THE HUSKY HERO

In the 1995 animated children's film, Balto is a wolf-dog mix with no friends. He saves the lives of sick children in the town of Nome in Alaska. The children have caught diphtheria and are very ill. It is winter, and there is a snowstorm that stops medicine from being brought to Nome by air or sea. Despite many challenges and dangers along the way, Balto manages to bring the medicine to the children by dog sled. He becomes a hero, and everyone, dogs and humans alike, love him and call him a hero.

Although the story has been changed to make it into an exciting film for children, Balto really did exist. Like in the movie, the real Balto was a sled dog who helped to save the sick children and adults of Nome during the diphtheria epidemic of 1925. The real Balto was a black and white Siberian husky and not a wolf dog mix. But there really was a snowstorm, and dogs really were the heroes of the story.

Balto was a six-year-old sled dog, born in 1919, who belonged to a Norwegian dog sled driver named Gunnar Kaasen. The diphtheria medicine that the people of Nome needed could not be sent from the Alaskan capital, Anchorage, by plane because the planes' engines were frozen. The railway line did not go as far as Nome, so the medicine could not go by train either. Therefore, the people of Nome decided to send teams of dog sleds to get the medicine from Anchorage, a journey of over 500 miles each way. The dogs and their sled drivers travelled cross country through a terrible snowstorm with strong winds and temperatures as low as 30 degrees centigrade below zero (-31°C/-23.8°F).

Balto was the lead dog in one of the dog sleds—the one who brought the medicine back safely to the people waiting in Nome.

The story became so well known that when Balto died in 1933, his body was taken to the Cleveland Museum of Natural History, where it can still be seen today. There is also a statue of Balto in New York City's Central Park.

The statue of Balto in Central Park, New York City

To this day, Balto is still one of the most famous dogs that ever lived in the United States.

REFLECTION

1. Look online for images of The Iditarod Trail Sled
   Dog Race (see https://iditarod.com/). Talk about
   what you can see in the photos or in the videos on
   the official website.
2. Find out more about the work of sled dogs. List one
   or two facts that you find.

CHAPTER 14

BOBI: THE OLDEST DOG IN THE WORLD

Some dogs have lived a very long time. Pebbles, a toy fox terrier from South Carolina in the United States, reached the grand old age of 22 years and seven months. She took the title of oldest dog in the world from a 21-year-old male chihuahua in Florida named TobyKeith. In January 2023, Spike, a chihuahua mix rescue dog from Ohio, claimed the Guinness World Record as the oldest dog in the world. He was 23 years old.

However, Spike did not hold the world record for very long–only two weeks. In February 2023, reports came of a much older dog in Portugal. After tests proved his incredible old age really was correct, 30-year-old Bobi claimed the record as the world's oldest dog.

He is not only the oldest dog alive, but he also is the oldest dog that ever lived. Bobi has lived his whole life on a farm in southern Portugal. Yet he nearly didn't live past puppyhood. It was only because his owner, who was an eight-year-old boy at the time, saved him and kept him hidden until his father agreed that the dog could stay with the family.

Bobi is a Portuguese livestock guardian dog, a brown Rafeiro de Alentejo. Dogs of this medium-size breed usually live to be about 12 or 14 years old. Bobi's mother lived until she was 18, so she was already older than was usual for the breed. No one really knows how Bobi has managed to live for over 31 years already. His age could be easily confirmed, as he was registered with a vet in 1992, and he is on a Portuguese pet database.

Bobi still lives with his owner, Leonel Costa, who is now 38. No one can say why Bobi has lived for so long. Leonel's only explanation is that Bobi has always had a calm and peaceful life on the farm. He has never been chained up, and he was never kept on a lead or leash. He eats normal human food, but with the spices washed off. He goes to the vet for regular checks, and apart from one time in 2018, he has always been healthy. Bobi grew up with lots of other animals too, so he was never alone.

These days, Bobi, who turned 31 in 2023, cannot see very well, and like many very old men, he likes to rest and sleep a lot in front of the fire.

Editor's Note: Unfortunately, as this book was going to press, we learned that Bobi passed away on October 21, 2023.

REFLECTION

1. The Dogs Trust charity in the United Kingdom says that "A dog is for life, not just for Christmas." Explain what this means. Do you agree or disagree?
2. What kinds of things do you think would help a dog live a long life? How many of those things would also help a human live a long life?

WANT TO READ MORE ABOUT DOGS?

If you enjoyed this book, you might also enjoy our fiction reader *Black Gold*, which features dogs. Now that you know a lot of dog vocabulary, it should be easier for you to read!

Benny is the best dog in the world. Just ask his owner, 15-year old Danny Brooks. Danny is not the best boy in the world—he's had trouble with the police, and he never has enough money. Danny's life as an orphan in the children's home is difficult, but as long as Benny is with him, he can be happy. So when something terrible happens to Benny, what will happen to Danny?

For information about this book and others, visit
https://www.wayzgoosepress.com/graded-readers/

Special Message from the Author

Thank you for buying this book. I hope you enjoyed reading it and that you have learnt something about dogs as well as improved your English skills.

I will be donating 20% of the royalties from this book to a dog rescue charity.

Galgos del Sol is a licensed charity based in Spain that rescues and rehomes galgos and podencos.

You can read more about their work helping hundreds of dogs each year make the journey from 'street life to sweet life' on their website and watch videos and reels on their excellent social media posts, in particular on Instagram and Facebook.

https://galgosdelsol.org/es/inicio/

So many dogs need our support, and it's almost impossible to choose one charity. That is why I support other dog rescue charities via micro-donations and Teaming. If you've never heard of this, the basic idea is that you give one euro (or the same amount in another currency) per month to each charity of your choice. You can support as many charities and social causes as you like (not only dog charities), but you only give one euro to each. One euro is not much; but when, for example, a thousand people donate one euro per month, it really makes a difference.

https://www.teaming.net/

My very best wishes to you and your four-legged friends,

Karen Richardson

About the Author

Dogs have always played a large part in my life. The first dog I remember well was Mandy, my grandparents' black and brown crossbreed. Equally as important to me as a small child was my favourite soft toy, a St. Bernard dog called Bernie.

When I was around 10 years old, my dad arrived home with a rescue dog, an 18-month-old greyhound called Blueit. Bluey (as we called her), had been trained for racing, but she wasn't good enough and needed a new home. She stayed with us until she died at the age of 11. Her best friend was my grandparents' next dog, a terrier cross called Lucky, also a rescue dog.

While my sister discovered her love of bull terriers, I continued to adopt sight hounds. We have two rescue dogs at the moment, Louie and Ivy. They are both Spanish greyhounds, also known as galgo Español. So far, Louie has lived with us for seven years, and Ivy has lived with us for five years.

Karen Richardson with Louie and Ivy

We don't know how old they are or what their previous lives were like, but they are wonderful companions for us and for each other. They love to have a good run twice a week, a walk every day, and regular sniffs around the garden. Apart from that, they spend a lot of their time snoozing on the sofa or on their beds next to me in my office.

Karen Richardson was born in England and moved to Germany in her late 20s, where she has been living and working in the English language teaching (ELT) industry ever since. For the past 20+ years, she has been teaching English in companies, for local authorities, and at colleges and universities in Germany. She has written coursebooks, teachers' guides, calendars, books for young learners, and a huge number of digital materials for large international publishers such as Macmillan Education, National Geographic Learning, and Pearson. She is the author of *How to Write Worksheets* (*https://eltteacher2writer.co.uk/our-books/how-to-write-work-sheets/*), published by ELT Teacher to Writer, and *Fifty Ways to Practice Business English*, published by Wayzgoose Press. She currently writes for *Business Spotlight* and *Spotlight*, monthly magazines published by the newspaper group Die Zeit for German-speaking learners of business English and general English.

Karen holds the Trinity Diploma TESOL as well as various teaching and intercultural trainer certificates. You can contact her via her website: http://www.compass-elt.com and follow her on Instagram on www.instagram.com/nature.words_

Made in the USA
Monee, IL
31 March 2024